AMONG THE LEAVES

WRITTEN BY THE GOOD AND THE BEAUTIFUL TEAM
DESIGNED BY KAYLA ELLINGSWORTH

© 2024 THE GOOD AND THE BEAUTIFUL, LLC
goodandbeautiful.com

Deciduous trees and evergreen trees are two of the most common types of trees found around the world.

DECIDUOUS TREES

Deciduous trees are characterized by their ability to shed their leaves in the fall. These trees often have robust trunks with branches that stretch out like fingers, adorned with thick foliage that provides shade and shelter during the hot summer months. When the seasons change and the temperatures begin to drop, the leaves of deciduous trees turn brilliant shades of yellow, orange, and red before eventually falling to the ground, creating a carpet of leaves underfoot. In the winter, deciduous trees are bare, revealing their intricate branching patterns against the stark white of the snow.

EVERGREEN TREES

In contrast, evergreen trees retain their foliage year-round, with thick needles or small, leathery leaves that are resistant to cold temperatures and harsh weather conditions. These trees provide a constant source of greenery even in the depths of winter, and their branches are often used as decoration during the winter holiday season. Evergreen trees can grow to be quite tall, with some reaching heights of over 30 m (100 ft). Their dense foliage provides shelter and nesting grounds for a wide range of animals, from squirrels and birds to deer and bears.

Deciduous and evergreen trees are an essential component of our ecosystem, providing vital oxygen, shelter, and food for a multitude of creatures. Their beauty and majesty have inspired artists, poets, and writers for centuries, and they continue to captivate and awe us with their stunning presence.

DECIDUOUS TREES

FRUIT-BEARING TREES (APPLE, PEAR, PEACH, FIG)

Fruit-bearing trees are a fascinating aspect of nature, with their ability to produce delicious, edible fruits that offer a feast for both the eyes and palate. These magnificent trees require a specific set of conditions to thrive, such as the right amount of sunlight, water, and nutrients. They also require consistent care, including pruning and fertilization, to ensure their optimal growth and fruit production.

Some fruit-bearing trees can produce fruit for several years, while others have a limited lifespan of fruit production. This is due to a variety of factors, including the age and health of the tree, as well as the amount of stress it endures. Fruit-bearing trees are a crucial component of our food system, providing a healthy and delicious source of sustenance for people worldwide. Their beautiful blooms and bountiful fruits are a reminder of the abundance and wonder of nature.

BANYAN TREES

DECIDUOUS

Banyan trees are awe-inspiring giants that tower over the landscape, their broad branches reaching out in every direction like the tentacles of a great sea creature. These trees are native to the tropical regions of Asia and can grow to be hundreds of years old, with some trees stretching up to 30 m (100 ft) tall.

One of the most remarkable features of the banyan tree is its aerial roots, which dangle from its branches like thick cords snaking their way down to the ground. These roots can grow to be several meters in diameter and are an important part of the tree's survival, allowing it to anchor itself to the soil and absorb moisture and nutrients from the earth. As the banyan tree matures, its trunk can become massive, with rough and gnarled bark that twists and turns like the contours of a labyrinth. Its leaves are large and shiny, with a vibrant green hue that stands out against the bright blue sky.

The banyan tree is also a symbol of spiritual significance in many cultures, revered for its longevity and perceived connection to the divine. It has been featured in many works of art and literature, and its majestic stature has inspired awe and wonder in people for centuries. The banyan tree is a remarkable specimen of the natural world, a towering giant that commands attention and admiration with its stunning beauty and imposing presence.

ASPEN TREES

DECIDUOUS

Aspen trees are a species found throughout North America. They are known for their striking white bark, which contrasts beautifully with their delicate green leaves that flutter in the slightest breeze. These trees are a relatively short-lived species, with a lifespan of about 50 to 70 years, but they grow quickly and can reach heights of up to 25 m (80 ft) tall. They typically grow in clusters, with multiple trunks sprouting from a single root system, giving them a unique and distinctive appearance.

The leaves of the aspen tree are small and round, with a soft, velvety texture that makes them pleasant to the touch. During the fall season, the leaves turn a brilliant yellow or gold, illuminating the landscape with their vibrant hues.

Aspen trees are an important part of many ecosystems, providing food and shelter for a wide variety of animals, including elk, deer, beavers, and birds. Their wood is also highly valued for its versatility and durability, making it ideal for use in a wide range of products, from furniture to paper. In addition to their practical uses, aspen trees have long held a special place in the cultural and spiritual traditions of many Native American nations. They are revered for their strength and resilience, as well as their ability to regenerate and renew themselves.

MAHOGANY TREES

DECIDUOUS

Mahogany trees are found in many parts of the world, particularly in the tropical regions of the Americas, Africa, and Asia. They are known for their dense reddish-brown wood, which is highly valued for its durability, beauty, and versatility. These stately trees can grow to be over 20 m (65 ft) tall and have a canopy that spreads out to over 15 m (50 ft) in diameter. Their leaves are large and shiny, with a deep green color that contrasts beautifully with the warm tones of their wood.

The wood of the mahogany tree is dense, hard, and resistant to decay, making it ideal for use in furniture, flooring, and other high-quality products. Its rich, reddish-brown color and fine grain give it a distinctive and luxurious look that is highly sought after by craftspeople and consumers alike. Sadly, mahogany trees are currently facing significant threats from overexploitation and habitat loss, as well as illegal logging and deforestation. Efforts are underway to protect and conserve these magnificent trees and ensure that they continue to thrive and flourish for generations to come.

BEECH TREES

Beech trees are found throughout many of the temperate regions of the world. They are known for their smooth gray bark and their leaves, which are typically oval-shaped with a pointed tip and a smooth, wavy edge. Beech trees can grow to be quite tall, reaching heights of up to 30 m (100 ft) or more, and they have a dense canopy that provides ample shade and beauty. During the fall season, their leaves turn a warm golden brown, creating a breathtaking display of color.

One of the most unique features of beech trees is their nuts, which are enclosed in a spiny, prickly husk and are a favorite food source for many animals, including squirrels, chipmunks, and birds. They are also known for their ability to grow in dense stands, forming extensive forests that support a rich and diverse range of plant and animal life.

BIRCH TREES

DECIDUOUS

Birch trees are charming and beloved tree species that are found throughout the northern regions of the world. One species, called the white birch, is known for its smooth white bark that peels away in thin layers to reveal a warm, golden-brown color underneath.

Birch trees have slender trunks with delicate, oval-shaped leaves that flutter in even the gentlest breeze and can reach heights of up to 25 m (80 ft) tall. During the fall season, their leaves turn a bright, vibrant yellow, adding a burst of color to the landscape.

In addition to their distinctive bark and leaves, birch trees are also known for their sap, which can be tapped and used to make a variety of products, including syrup. They are also known for their ability to grow in cold, harsh environments, making them a valuable and resilient species in many northern regions of the world.

CHERRY TREES

Cherry trees are an exquisite and beloved tree species known for their vibrant, showy blossoms and delicious fruit. They are native to many parts of the world, including Asia, Europe, and North America, and are highly valued for their ornamental and culinary uses. Cherry trees can grow to be up to 9 m (30 ft) tall, with a broad, spreading canopy that is covered in stunning pink or white blossoms during the spring season. Their leaves are dark green and glossy, with a distinctly pointed shape that adds to their overall charm and appeal.

In addition to their striking appearance, cherry trees are also known for their delicious fruit, which is often used in pies, jams, and other sweet treats. Cherries come in a variety of colors, ranging from deep red to golden yellow, and are highly prized for their juicy, sweet flavor. They are also valued for their cultural significance, with cherry blossom festivals and traditions celebrated in many parts of the world.

The American chestnut tree was once one of the most beloved and valuable tree species in North America. These stately trees could grow to over 30 m (100 ft) tall and had broad, spreading canopies that provided ample shade and beauty. They were known for their delicious nuts, which were a favorite food source for many animals as well as humans.

AMERICAN CHESTNUT TREES

DECIDUOUS

Sadly, the American chestnut tree has been largely wiped out due to a devastating fungal disease known as chestnut blight. The disease was first discovered in the early 1900s and quickly spread throughout the United States, killing millions of chestnut trees and devastating the landscape. Efforts are currently underway to restore the American chestnut tree population through hybridization and genetic engineering. These efforts offer hope for the future of this beloved species and a chance to restore the once-great American chestnut tree to its rightful place as a treasured part of our natural world.

COTTONWOOD TREES

DECIDUOUS

Cottonwood trees are found throughout North America, Europe, and Asia. They are known for their lofty size, with some reaching heights of up to 30 m (100 ft) tall. One of the most distinctive features of cottonwood trees is their leaves, which are large and triangular in shape, with a vibrant, bright green color. In the fall, their leaves turn a stunning yellow, adding a burst of color to the autumn landscape. Cottonwood trees are also known for their distinctive, fluffy seeds, which resemble cotton and are carried by the wind to help them spread.

Cottonwood trees are also highly valued for their wood, which is used for a variety of purposes, including furniture and paper products. In addition to their practical uses, cottonwood trees are cherished for their cultural and historical significance. They have played an important role in many Native American cultures, and their bark and leaves have been used for medicinal purposes for centuries.

MAGNOLIA TREES

DECIDUOUS

Magnolia trees are a breathtaking and beloved tree species renowned for their stunning and flamboyant flowers and distinctive aroma. They are indigenous to various regions of the world, including Asia and the Americas, and are esteemed for their ornamental and therapeutic uses. Magnolia trees can tower up to 25 m (80 ft) tall, with a broad, far-reaching canopy draped in magnificent, aromatic blooms during the spring season. Their leaves are sizable, glossy, and dark green, providing a lush and verdant backdrop to their magnificent flowers.

Apart from their striking appearance, magnolia trees are valued for their medicinal properties. The bark and leaves of the magnolia tree have been used in traditional medicine to treat a range of health issues, including anxiety, depression, and digestive disorders. They also have cultural significance, with magnolia blossoms often used in weddings and religious ceremonies.

The magnolia tree is so cherished in the state of Mississippi that it is the official state tree.

ELM TREES

DECIDUOUS

The stately elm tree once thrived throughout North America, loved for its striking long branches and immense shade. However, around 1930, Dutch elm disease was introduced unintentionally from Europe, possibly by imported timber. Dutch elm disease is a fungus that is most often spread by insects such as the bark beetle. Since then, many species of elm trees have been declining.

There are more than 30 species of elm trees throughout the world; however, most of them are in the northern regions of Europe, Asia, and North America. Elm trees can grow tall, usually about 15 to 20 m (50 to 70 ft), and some can grow over 30 m (100 ft). The fruit of an elm tree is called a samara. It often has flat "wings" on either side to help carry it on the wind to other places to take root. Elm leaves are toothed and uniquely lopsided, with one side of each base longer than the other.

Elm wood is very valuable, especially for making boats, because it is still durable when underwater. In the past it was even used to make water pipes in England. Slippery elm is also believed to have medicinal properties for ailments, including sore throats.

HAWTHORN TREES

As you might expect from the name, a distinguishing feature of most types of hawthorn is the thorns that grow from the trunk and branches. In some varieties, such as the American cockspur hawthorn, these thorns can be up to 8 cm (3 in) long! Historically, this tree has been a popular choice for planting in hedges since its formidable prickles and tendency to grow into dense thickets create a natural fence to keep livestock in and intruders out. The name hawthorn even comes from Middle English words meaning "thorn of the hedge."

We can learn more about this tree from another of its common names, the thornapple. As this name suggests, the hawthorn is actually related to both apples and roses, as all of these plants are members of the Rosaceae family. Hawthorns bear clusters of white or pink five-petaled flowers and produce red fruit. Commonly called a berry, this fruit is like a cross between a rosehip and an apple. Wildlife and humans both enjoy hawthorn fruit, which is often made into jam. This tree is found throughout the temperate zones of the Northern Hemisphere.

Tales of the American folk hero Paul Bunyan describe him using a spiky hawthorn branch for a back scratcher, a detail that humorously highlights the strength and toughness of this gigantic lumberjack. Americans have also appreciated the more delicate aspects of this tree: Missouri chose the roselike hawthorn blossom as its state flower.

In the midst of a sun-kissed meadow, the locust tree stands tall. Its delicate, fernlike leaves cast a lacy pattern of shadows on the ground below as birds, bees, and butterflies seek refuge in the shade. This deciduous tree is primarily found in the central and eastern regions of the United States. Standing tall at heights ranging from 12 to 30 m (40 to 100 ft), it boasts a sturdy trunk covered in furrowed bark.

LOCUST TREES

From late spring to early summer, the locust tree bursts into a floral display of cream-white blossoms, emitting a sweet fragrance. As the flowering season concludes, seedpods develop, housing small, hard seeds that remain on the tree through the winter. Highly adaptable with a rapid growth rate, the locust tree is favored for reforestation, landscaping, and erosion control. Care must be taken when introducing this tree, as it can become invasive in certain areas due to its large, aggressive root system.

HICKORY TREES

DECIDUOUS

Eighteen different species of hickory trees—all part of the larger walnut family—grow across North America and eastern Asia. Hickory trees, like other walnuts, produce a drupe, or fruit, with a nutlike pit inside. Many people are familiar with the shagbark hickory tree and its edible "nut." (You can probably guess how the shagbark gets its name.) But did you know the pecan tree is actually a species of hickory? The pecan tree grows a fleshy drupe that has a hard seed inside. Crack open the seed, and inside is what we know as pleasant-tasting pecans. The pignut hickory tree is an exception when it comes to tasty "nuts." Its seeds taste so bad that only pigs would want to eat them.

Hickory leaves are compound, meaning many smaller leaflets are attached to a single stem. The flowers of hickory trees are distinctive as well. Male flowers grow as long, lime-green catkins, which are strings of flowers clustered along a thin body. As the catkins fall in late spring to early summer, they are eaten by birds and squirrels or have their nectar consumed by pollinating insects. At the same time, pollen from these male flowers makes its way into the air and then lands on the female flowers, which are much shorter catkins. Perhaps you have seen these stringy catkins on the ground, cars, or sidewalks near a hickory tree.

While most hickory trees are monoecious [muh-NEE-shus], meaning that each tree has both male and female flowers, some species, including the shagbark hickory, are dioecious [di-EE-shus], meaning each tree has only male flowers or only female flowers.

MAPLE TREES

DECIDUOUS

When people think of a tree, they often think of the mighty maple. It's no wonder, as at least 120 species grow around the world in almost all temperate climates. The maple's classic tree shape, with a substantial round crown of leaves atop a strong, straight trunk, makes it stand out. Its leaf shape, too, is unmistakable. Three main points, or lobes, emanate out from the leaf's petiole, or stem.

Maple hardwood is both striking and solid, making it popular for crafting furniture, flooring, cabinets, and more. The sweetest use of maple trees is a tasty one: maple syrup. Maple trees produce abundant, sweet sap that serves as their source of energy. By tapping a small hole into the trunk of an especially sweet species, such as the sugar maple, sugarmakers can collect sap to produce this delicious food.

Pollinators appreciate maple trees, too. As one of the earliest trees to flower each spring, maples produce tiny flowers that serve as a food source for bees and other nectar-loving insects.

OAK TREES

DECIDUOUS

Oaks can be one of the simpler trees to identify, as many varieties have leaves with a distinct lobed shape. Within this basic shape, many variations exist: the sharp, deeply separated lobes of the scarlet oak have an almost lacy appearance, while southern red oaks produce leaves with only a few thick, rounded lobes. Not all oaks have lobed leaves, however. The live oak has rounded oval leaves with smooth margins, and the laurel oak has long, pointed, oval leaves with serrated margins.

One feature that is easy to recognize among all oak trees is their nut, the acorn! Acorns can be round, oval, or pointed, but the cap at one end readily distinguishes them from the nuts of other trees. If you spot a tree with acorns, you've almost certainly found an oak, no matter what shape its leaves are.

Because oak wood is hard and water-resistant, it is ideal for building houses, furniture, and even barrels for storing liquid. Cork comes from the outer bark of the cork oak, an evergreen type of oak from the Mediterranean area. Historically, oaks were important for the production of iron gall ink. In the Middle Ages, this ink was created from abnormal growths, called galls, caused when certain insects lay their eggs in oak leaf buds.

The oak is one of the most common varieties of tree in North America, so it's no wonder that types of oak are claimed as state trees by six US states—Connecticut, Georgia, Illinois, Iowa, Maryland, and New Jersey. This impressive tree, which can reach over 30 m (100 ft) in height, is also a fitting choice for the national tree of the United States. On your next nature walk, see how many varieties of oak you can spot!

SASSAFRAS TREES

DECIDUOUS

Bears, deer, woodchucks, rabbits, birds, and butterflies all agree that a sassafras tree is a great place to find food—and for good reason. While many of these animals like to eat the drupes, or berrylike fruit, of sassafras trees, people have also found many uses for these unique, sweet-smelling, and fast-growing trees found throughout the eastern United States.

A quick way to identify a sassafras tree is by looking at its leaves. The leaves on this tree can be oval, mitten shaped, or lobed, with two to five lobes per leaf. One tree can contain all of these different leaf shapes, making it easy to identify a sassafras tree. However, most people know a sassafras tree because of its sweet smells. These trees have lovely scented leaves, bark, roots, and golden-yellow blossoms, with smells similar to root beer and lemon. It's no surprise then that sassafras trees have edible parts. Leaves can be eaten or used to thicken soups and stews like gumbo, and the roots of the sassafras tree have been used to make, you guessed it, root beer! Native Americans even used sassafras trees to make teas and medicines for illnesses like the common cold.

Look for the vibrant leaves of the sassafras tree in the fall when they turn bright colors of orange, red, yellow, or purple.

WALNUT TREES

DECIDUOUS

Have you ever eaten walnuts in a salad? Or maybe you like them in a dessert like ice cream or chocolate, or on their own as a healthy snack. However you like to eat them, walnuts can be a nutritious addition to a healthy diet.

An interesting fact is that walnuts come from trees! Walnut trees can be found in many places around the world: North and South America, Europe, Asia, and the West Indies. There are about 20 different species of walnut trees, each with compound leaves containing 5 to 23 leaflets. Two of the most common are the black walnut and the English walnut. Other species include the California black walnut, Japanese walnut, and Persian walnut.

Walnuts come from the drupes, or fruit, of the walnut tree. Inside the drupe is a hard shell where the walnuts, or seeds, can be found. In the early American colonies, settlers found many uses for walnuts, adding them to soups, grinding them up for flour, or storing them over the winter for a long-lasting snack. There is one catch, however, when harvesting walnuts. Black walnut drupes, although they are green in color, contain an herbicide that can stain hands and clothing black. Once the husk and shell are removed, the walnuts can be eaten or left out to dry. The drupes will begin falling off the tree when they are ripe.

Throughout history people have made expensive furniture out of the wood from walnut trees. You may even have a walnut desk or table in your home.

There are many varieties of willows—over 400—and they vary greatly in size! Some grow tall, up to 30 m (100 ft), and others are rather small and shrublike. Willows grow in many places around the world and often prefer cool areas. Willows also have deep, strong roots and are sometimes planted to prevent or help stop erosion.

Willow wood is rather light but is tough and helpful in making things like doors, baseball bats, and even tool handles. The small branches can be a variety of colors, such as red, orange, or yellow. Certain types of willows contain salicin, which can be used to produce salicylic acid, an ingredient that is in some pain relievers. Willows also have narrow green leaves that alternate on branches. Catkins—small clusters of flowers or blossoms—appear on the trees, usually in late winter or early spring.

WILLOW TREES

DECIDUOUS

Perhaps one of the most familiar and graceful willows, with its gorgeous, long, slender branches that cascade from the top and almost reach the ground, is the mesmerizing weeping willow tree. These and other varieties of willows grow to about 9 to 12 m (30 to 40 ft) and often have a spread of the same size. Because of this, these willows can be a wonderful source of shade and a lovely place to climb up and read a good book!

DOGWOOD TREES

DECIDUOUS

Dogwood can refer to many species of trees and shrubs found in the Northern Hemisphere. In the United States, dogwood usually refers to the flowering dogwood tree, a native species that is especially prized for its dramatic white or pink "flowers" that can be 8 to 13 cm (3 to 5 in) across. However, what look like four-petaled blooms are in fact bracts, or special leaves, that surround the actual flowers, which are a cluster of tiny greenish-yellow blossoms. (You probably know another plant with colorful bracts surrounding small flowers: the poinsettia!)

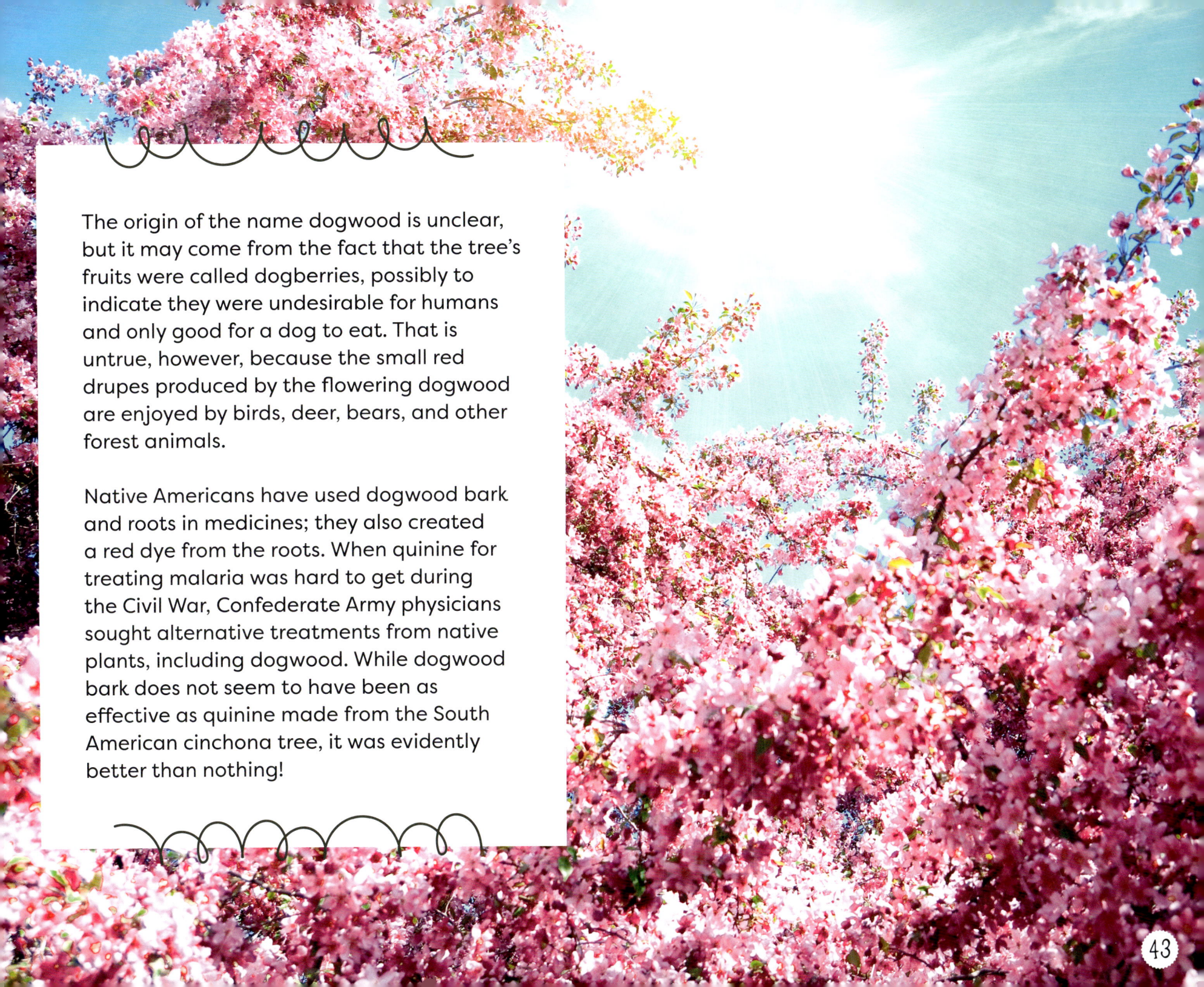

The origin of the name dogwood is unclear, but it may come from the fact that the tree's fruits were called dogberries, possibly to indicate they were undesirable for humans and only good for a dog to eat. That is untrue, however, because the small red drupes produced by the flowering dogwood are enjoyed by birds, deer, bears, and other forest animals.

Native Americans have used dogwood bark and roots in medicines; they also created a red dye from the roots. When quinine for treating malaria was hard to get during the Civil War, Confederate Army physicians sought alternative treatments from native plants, including dogwood. While dogwood bark does not seem to have been as effective as quinine made from the South American cinchona tree, it was evidently better than nothing!

ASH TREES

DECIDUOUS

The ash tree is a large, sturdy tree found in many forests and landscapes. Its rough bark adds a rugged charm to its appearance, reflecting the tree's age and endurance. In spring, the ash tree sprouts fresh green leaves that form a dense, vibrant canopy. Birds take advantage of this lush shelter to build their nests and fill the air with cheerful songs. During the hot summer months, the ash tree provides cool shade, offering a welcome escape from the scorching sun.

As autumn arrives, the ash tree undergoes a stunning transformation. Its leaves turn various shades of yellow, gold, and red, creating a vivid spectacle of colors. These leaves eventually fall to the ground, forming a crisp carpet that crunches underfoot. Despite its allure, the ash tree faces a serious threat from the emerald ash borer, an insect that poses a danger to the tree's survival.

EVERGREEN TREES

EUCALYPTUS TREES

High up in the top of a tree in Australia, a koala munches away on tough, leathery leaves. These are the leaves of the lovely-smelling eucalyptus, sometimes called the gum tree. A waxy coating on the leaves helps hold in water even in Australia's dry bushlands, so much so that koalas do not need to drink and instead get much of their water from eating enough eucalyptus.

Koalas aren't the only living things that rely on the eucalyptus. The long leaves are also rich with oils that can be used for healing aches, clearing up congestion, and keeping mosquitoes away. Old trees can form hollow sections that become homes to possums, parrots, bats, and even bees. The bark from some species of these fast-growing trees can be made into paper, and their wood can be made into fences and building materials.

Not only is eucalyptus a fast-growing tree family, it is also one of the tallest. A swamp gum tree on Australia's island of Tasmania is so tall at 100 m (330 ft) that it has its own name, Centurion.

Aside from Australia, eucalyptus is native to other Pacific islands. In the Philippines the rainbow eucalyptus reveals an array of splendid colors when its bark begins to peel.

FIR TREES

EVERGREEN

If you have ever had a live Christmas tree in your home, there's a good chance it was a fir. Balsam and Fraser firs, both native to the eastern US, are two of the most popular choices for Christmas decor. You'd need a really big living room to fit a full-grown tree, though: when mature, these two firs can reach 15 to 21 m (50 to 70 ft). Other American varieties of fir found westward from the Rocky Mountains can get even taller. The white fir, noble fir, and Pacific silver fir all tower up to 60 m (200 ft)!

Firs can be distinguished from other evergreen conifers, or cone-bearing trees, by their needles, which are flat and soft (rather than stiff and sharp, like the needles of a spruce). Like other conifers, firs are sticky trees, oozing resin from spots on their trunks. Resin, which is different from sap, helps protect the tree from disease, acting like a scab to keep out insects and fungus. This gooey substance doesn't dissolve in water, which is why you would have to use oil or alcohol to clean it off your skin, clothes, or hair. Not all resin is sticky, however: amber is resin from ancient trees that has fossilized into a beautiful gem!

The main or dominant tree in many old-growth forests is the pyramid-shaped hemlock. A tall tree that can live in deep woods, it has short, wide, dark green needles that grow in lines along thin twigs. Creatures of the woodlands depend on hemlocks for habitat and food. Tiny seed-bearing cones grow from the tips of branches. In turn, chipmunks, voles, and other rodents feed on the hemlock seeds once they are released. Hemlock needles and new growth provide fodder for large animals such as moose and deer and sometimes smaller mammals such as porcupines. Even certain fish, including trout, need hemlock trees for survival: the strong, dense branches provide plenty of shade to keep the waters below nice and cool for these fish.

HEMLOCK TREES

EVERGREEN

The longest-living trees on the West Coast of the US are the great redwood trees, but it is the eastern hemlock tree that lives the longest on the East Coast of the US and in Canada—usually about 500 years. Across this region, a six-legged problem infests these aged trees: an insect called the hemlock woolly adelgid [uh–DEL–jid]. The adelgid lays eggs on the underside of hemlock needles and covers the eggs with a woollike material. In just 4 to 10 years, these insects can destroy a tree.

PINE TREES

EVERGREEN

Many evergreen trees have needles. Many produce cones. But only one kind of tree has needles that grow in clusters: the pine. Pine needles are predictable with two, three, or five needles per bundle. The number of needles that appear in each cluster is a clue to the specific species. White pine trees have five needles (remember this by noting that the word *white* has five letters), yellow pines have three needles, and red pines have two needles. Within those pine types are more than 120 different species, ranging from the popular eastern white pine that was often made into ship masts to the stately longleaf pine that stands tall throughout the southern US.

We know that all plants need water, oxygen, sunlight, and nutrients to grow, but there is one more unique need that many pines have for regeneration. That need is fire. With strong pine cones glued shut by their own resin, some pine species need fire to break through the cones so that the seeds can escape. The scraggly jack pine is one such tree. Jack pine cones can stay shut for years until a fire comes through.

Pine is a softwood perfect for building and for making pulp that is turned into paper. There's a good chance you are holding pine in your hand as you read this book.

Juniper Trees

If you walk past a juniper tree, the first thing you may notice is its wonderful, sharp, spicy fragrance. However, while humans find the aroma pleasing, some insects do not, so a chest made of juniper wood can keep moths away from woolen clothes!

Found across the Northern Hemisphere in North America, Europe, Africa, Asia, and even the Arctic, junipers are a popular choice for beautifying gardens and landscapes. Depending on the variety, junipers may be tall, stately trees or low, branching shrubs. In the US, the eastern red cedar is a type of juniper that can grow up to 12 to 15 m (40 to 50 ft) high in the shape of a cone; however, the variety known as the common juniper is considered a shrub because it can remain under 4 m (15 ft) and be nearly as wide as it is tall. You might have encountered an even tinier juniper if you've ever seen a bonsai tree. Junipers are an excellent choice for this ancient Asian art form that creates miniature potted trees through careful and artistic pruning.

Their prickly leaves can be shaped like needles or scales, and many kinds of juniper have both. Juniper flowers are either male or female, and often a single tree bears only one kind of flower, meaning that more than one tree is needed for pollination to occur. Junipers are a type of conifer, meaning that their reddish or blue "berries" are actually a type of cone! These cones are often used to add flavor to foods or drinks. Juniper cones are a traditional spice for softening the strong flavor of game meats such as venison. Native Americans have also used these cones in medicines.

Imagine standing in the middle of a forest filled with evergreen spruce trees, flurries of snow falling all around and landing softly on the whorled branches. What a beautiful sight that would be! Spruce trees are another type of evergreen tree, characterized by scaly bark and a pyramid shape. Unlike pine needles, spruce needles are attached individually. There are around 40 species of spruce trees found in the Northern Hemisphere of the earth, some of which can live more than 600 years. In fact, a spruce tree in Sweden named Old Tjikko is said to be over 9,000 years old!

SPRUCE TREES

EVERGREEN

Many of these spruce species have fascinating uses. White spruce and Engelmann spruce make good lumber and timber, while Norway and Serbian spruce make good Christmas trees. The Wright brothers' famous first aircraft was made from spruce trees, and some instruments like guitars, mandolins, and violins also contain spruce wood. In addition, spruce trees are used to make paper, their shoots are a good source of vitamin C, and Native Americans made baskets from their flexible roots. Talk about some useful trees!

There is one part of a spruce tree, however, that can have its disadvantages. The resin of spruce trees is highly flammable and can cause forest fires. Although forest fires can sometimes be good for ecosystems, they can be dangerous for nearby towns or neighborhoods.

REDWOOD TREES

Even though it begins as a seed no bigger than a watermelon seed, the magnificent redwood can grow to be one of the tallest trees on the earth, growing over 91 m (300 ft) tall! Some redwoods also live over 2,000 years, although most live about 600 years, which is still incredibly long!

Redwoods were designed to last long due to their "armor"! The reddish color of their bark and heartwood, which is how they got their name, is from high tannin levels. This tannin, along with other chemicals found in their bark, helps fight off fungal diseases and is a type of insect pesticide. In addition, their bark holds large amounts of water and contains low resin. This forms a natural fire protection, allowing them to survive even some of the hottest forest fires!

Many animals make their homes in redwood trees. The threatened marbled murrelet—a small seabird—nests in moist forests such as the redwood groves off the coast of the Pacific Ocean. The female murrelet lays just one egg high in a redwood tree on a small mat of moss. Other animals can spend their entire lives in the redwood trees. One such animal, the wandering salamander, glides from one tree to another and may never touch the ground. Redwoods are a valuable resource to our biosphere!

MONKEY PUZZLE TREES

EVERGREEN

When we hear of national monuments, we often think of grand geological wonders, towering statues, or stately historical buildings. In the country of Chile, one national monument is a tree. The monkey puzzle tree is so special and endangered that, in order to protect it from logging, it was given this title.

A species of conifer, or cone-bearing tree, the monkey puzzle tree looks as strange as its name sounds. Its needles are stiff triangles that grow in a spiral pattern around branches that come out of the trunk in groups of five. Some say the needles look like reptile scales. With a trunk that looks like pineapple scales and a base that looks like an elephant's foot, the monkey puzzle tree got its name when a person said that climbing it would be a puzzle even for a monkey.

Even the cones are wild looking. Male cones, which produce pollen, are about the size of a cucumber and are spiky. Female cones, though, are huge, as big as a pineapple or larger. Each female cone has about 200 seeds or nuts inside. These nuts are an important food for some native people of South America, especially the Mapuche people, who live in the Andes Mountains. The nuts can be eaten raw, boiled, roasted, ground into flour, or fermented to make a beverage.

CYPRESS TREES

EVERGREEN

Where there are cypress trees, there is often water, and where there are cypress trees growing in water, the water becomes clean. While cypress trees can grow in dry soil, many of them find their homes in wetlands, where they absorb pollutants from the environment.

Cypress needles are quite different from the needles of other cone-bearing trees. The needles appear flat, feel soft, and even look lacy or feathery. It's their clean, woodsy odor that makes smelling the needles refreshing—except for the Arizona cypress. The oil in this tree's needles smells like a skunk. Cypress bark grows in long ridges that come off in stringy strips on most species. Oils in the tree make the wood resistant to rotting, making it good for building boats and decks.

Many cypress trees are quite old, living to 500 or 600 years. While some are evergreen, keeping their needles year-round, others actually lose their needles in the fall. The bald cypress gets its name from this deciduous leaf-dropping habit.

CEDAR TREES

EVERGREEN

Just as our skin changes and wrinkles with age, the bark of a cedar tree does the same! Smooth grayish-brown bark is found on young cedar trees. But as they age, their bark turns brown and cracked and even a bit scaly. Cedar trees can grow to be quite large, over 30 m (100 ft) tall, and can have a trunk up to 3 m (10 ft) in diameter.

The leaves of cedars are three-sided needles that grow in clusters scattered along the branches. Each leaf lives on the tree from three to six years and has two resin tubes. Also growing on short stalks of the cedar tree are lovely green or purple cones that contain resin. These hold the cedar seeds and are protected by small wood scales that wrap around the barrel-shaped cones.

The wood from cedar trees is lightweight and soft. It also secretes resin that helps protect the tree from insects or disease. It is very durable, even when it comes in contact with water or soil. These attributes make it a great source for building material and an important resource in some areas of the world. The strong aroma of cedar trees is produced during the distillation of the wood; this is done by heating the cedarwood, which releases the vapors. Because of its strong, woody scent, cedarwood is used in many things today, such as closet linings, chests, perfumes, and toiletries.

Southern live oaks are pretty unique in that they are nearly evergreen and have leaves all throughout the year! They drop their leaves over a few weeks in late winter and early spring, but the new leaves have already grown, so the trees are never bare. Shiny, deep green leaves are coated with a thick layer of wax, and the edges often curl under. Both the waxy layer and the curling help the leaves retain moisture on hot summer days.

Southern live oaks are large trees. They can grow up to 18 m (60 ft) tall, but their crowns can extend to twice that distance. One of the largest southern live oaks has a crown of nearly 46 m (150 ft)! That is a lot of shade! Their long, sweeping branches droop and sometimes even reach the ground. When planting a live oak, it's important to give it lots of room, as it will often upend sidewalks or foundations of structures that are too close.

SOUTHERN LIVE OAK TREES

The wood from the southern live oak is very valuable. It is extremely durable due to its density and strength. Its wood is also decay and disease resistant and is among the heaviest wood in North America, weighing about 27 kg (60 lb) per cubic foot when it is dried. In fact, "Old Ironsides" was a nickname given to the naval vessel *USS Constitution* due to the immense strength of its live oak wood, which survived repeated cannon firing during the War of 1812.

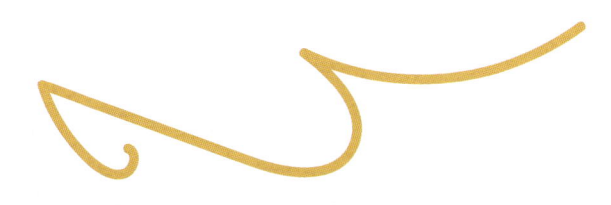

HOLLY TREES

For many people, the holly tree brings to mind Christmas cards and festive carols. Indeed, holly's association with midwinter celebrations goes back to ancient Celtic and Roman cultures. Early Christians borrowed the practice of decorating with holly boughs, turning what was once a pagan tradition into a symbol of Christian belief: the thorns became a representation of Christ's crown of thorns and the red berries His shed blood, while the green leaves in winter symbolized eternal life.

The spiny green leaves and bright red berries that we recognize from Christmas decorations belong to a European variety known as English holly. American holly, found in the eastern US, has a similar appearance. In fact, Delaware values these trees so much that it adopted the American holly as its state tree. Both English and American holly trees can grow to be around 15 m (50 ft) tall.

However, the holly family contains many more varieties than the ones we know from Christmas cards. Holly grows throughout the world, thriving especially in mountainous parts of the tropics. This tree typically has oval leaves, and in addition to red, its berries can be white, yellow, pink, or black. Some varieties common to the US go by names such as Carolina holly, catberry, and common winterberry. We even know that George Washington grew this last variety, and today you can still see common winterberry growing in the Mount Vernon gardens. Hawaii also has its own native variety of holly called Aiea. And if you've ever tried the popular South American beverage yerba mate, you've tasted a tea made from the leaves of a holly plant!

BLUEBERRY ASH TREES

EVERGREEN

Despite what its name suggests, the blueberry ash tree is not closely related to the ash tree common to the Northern Hemisphere. A member of a family of tropical trees and shrubs, the blueberry ash is native to eastern Australia.

With its pretty blossoms and fruit, the blueberry ash is a favorite decorative tree and can be found in gardens and along city streets. Because its fringed, bell-shaped flowers in white or pink resemble tiny skirts, another common name for this tree is fairy petticoat. Its vibrant blue fruit is not truly a berry, but a drupe like an olive or cherry. The fruit can remain on the plant throughout the year, with the charming result that "berries" and blooms appear on the plant at the same time. The blooms smell like licorice.

While many types of birds enjoy the fruit of the blueberry ash, the male regent bowerbird does something even more interesting with the colorful fruit: he uses it when courting a mate! To attract females, male regent bowerbirds build a bower, an elaborate structure of sticks decorated with colorful items including shells, fruit, and even pieces of plastic. These birds are especially drawn to the color blue, and one might say the blueberry ash fruit fits the bill perfectly.

PALM TREES

EVERGREEN

A palm with a slender, arching trunk topped by a cluster of broad, waving fronds is one of the most recognizable symbols of tropical places, and with good reason: palms are most prolific in tropical regions within 30 degrees north or south of the equator.

Palms really grow more like grasses than trees. Unlike woody trees, whose trunks and branches continue to grow wider as the tree ages, palms grow from a single point on the stem. This means that they reach their full width before growing upwards by adding new leaves at the top of the trunk. As old leaves die and fall off, part of the leaf stalks are left behind to become a new section of the trunk. In some palms, the dead leaves stay attached, creating a "skirt" of dead leaves surrounding the trunk.

Palm leaves are called fronds and come in two main shapes. In palmate fronds, the leaf parts are arranged in a circular pattern that resembles a fan. In pinnate fronds, leaf parts are arranged in a feather shape down both sides of a central stem. Palm trunks can vary in size. The long, slender trunk of the Colombian Quindío wax palm can reach 60 m (197 ft). In contrast, the bush palmetto found in the southern US often has no trunk visible above ground, though its fronds can reach about $2\frac{1}{2}$ m (8 ft).

Palms are often important to local cultures and economies; their fruit provides food, while leaves and trunks furnish material for building houses and fibers for making baskets and textiles. Even if you don't live where palms grow, you still may have eaten a palm fruit in the form of a date or a coconut! The date was probably grown in the Middle East, Africa, or California, and the coconut might have come from India, the Philippines, or Indonesia.

South Carolina is known as the Palmetto State, and it joins Florida in claiming the Sabal palmetto as the official state tree. The palmetto also appears on the South Carolina state flag.

PEPPERMINT TREES

EVERGREEN

The peppermint—or peppy tree, as it is called by local Australians—takes its name from the refreshing peppermint scent of its long, narrow leaves. A type of myrtle, it belongs to the same family as another well-known Australian tree, the eucalyptus. Myrtles are tropical trees known for the fragrant oil produced in their leaves, and include the guava, clove, and bay rum (whose leaves are the source of a classic cologne fragrance).

Called the *Wonnil* in the Noongar language, this tree has long been used for medicine by Aboriginal Australian people. Its strong fragrance makes it ideal for treating congestion, and the leaves can be made into tea. It can also be used as an antiseptic for cleaning and dressing wounds.

The elegant pendular, or weeping, shape of its branches has also given this tree the name willow myrtle. In the spring, its sweet white blossoms are the favorite of bees and other insects. Some cultivars (plants carefully grown by humans to keep specific traits) have decorative purple, red, or cream-colored leaves, making the peppy tree a perfect choice for gardens.

KUMQUAT TREES

EVERGREEN

This charming tree with glossy green leaves and small orange-yellow fruit is a member of the Rutaceae family, which includes citrus like lemons, limes, oranges, and grapefruit. While other citrus fruits are typically peeled before eating, the kumquat fruit can be eaten whole with the skin on. With its sweet, pulpy skin and tart, juicy interior, a kumquat fruit is like nature's own sweet-and-sour candy! The fruit can also be cooked or made into jam, and in Asia, it is traditionally preserved in syrup or salt.

Originating in East Asia, these trees were brought to Europe in 1846 and then to America. Today they are grown around the world in sub-tropical regions. Mature trees typically reach 2 to 4 m (8 to 12 ft) in height. Their small white flowers and cheerful golden fruit make them popular ornamental trees, and given enough sunlight, they can even thrive indoors. With their abundance of fruit, kumquat trees are enjoyed as a symbol of prosperity and good luck as part of the Chinese New Year celebration. Kumquat trees or boughs are also sometimes used as Christmas decorations.

With leaves of a striking deep green on the top and an almost shimmery silver on the underside, the olive tree is truly lovely. It has been around for thousands of years; in 3500 BC it grew on the island of Crete in the Mediterranean. Olives and olive oil are a major part of the cuisine in this part of the world.

OLIVE TREES

EVERGREEN

The olive tree is an evergreen that most often has many branches that appear to twist around the trunk. Olive trees reach anywhere from 3 to 12 m (10 to 40 ft) high, but they are slow growers. It isn't until 15 to 20 years of growth that they are considered full producers, although they can begin growing fruit at around four years. Another incredible thing is that a new trunk will begin to grow out of the roots if the top of the tree dies off. The olive tree wood is also decay resistant. Both of these traits play a part in how olive trees have such a long life span, with some people believing they can live up to 1,500 years!

Olives and olive trees are even used as a teaching tool in the Bible. The oil from olives is very valuable as nourishment and medicine and has been a vital part of many cultures for a long time.